D1498644

LIVING ON GOD'S
ECONOMY

Ten Reasons *to* Place Your Financial
Hope *in the* Promises *of* God

PAUL CHAPPELL

First published in 2009 by Striving Together Publications, a ministry
of Lancaster Baptist Church, Lancaster, CA 93535. Striving Together
Publications is committed to providing tried, trusted, and proven
books that will further equip local churches to carry out the Great
Commission. Your comments and suggestions are valued.

Striving Together Publications
4020 E. Lancaster Blvd.
Lancaster, CA 93535
800.201.7748
www.strivingtogether.com

Cover design by Andrew Jones
Layout by Craig Parker
Edited by Monica Bass, Cary Schmidt, and Tina Butterfield
Special thanks to our proofreaders.

ISBN 978-1-59894-082-4

Printed in the United States of America

Table of Contents

Dedication

Apart from the inner working of the Holy Spirit to produce a desire for giving within my own heart, no person has instructed me in a greater way concerning how to live on God's economy than Dr. Don Sisk.

Dr. Sisk is a missionary statesman who has preached in over sixty-five countries, founded churches and a Bible college in Japan, and formerly served as the director of Baptist International Missions, Inc.

When Dr. Sisk began preaching about missions at Lancaster Baptist Church, we supported two missionaries. As of this writing, Lancaster Baptist Church supports over 180 missionaries with nearly one million dollars annually. Dr. Sisk has been used of God through his teaching, his joy in living, and his example in giving to show us how to live on God's economy. As an individual Christian and as a pastor, I am grateful for his influence on my life and the lives of those of us at the Lancaster Baptist Church.

Introduction

Have you ever noticed how unpredictable economies of men can be? As I write these pages, the American economy is facing one of its worst downturns in the last century. The stock market has lost significant value over recent months, the government has bailed out major financial institutions in unprecedented ways, and a new administration is instituting the country's largest ever "stimulus package" of financial expenditures.

As of this writing, unemployment in our country is nearing nine percent, up significantly from just a year ago, and many Americans are facing significant losses from risky mortgages and real estate gambles gone bad. Spending is down in every sector, and economies around the globe are facing similar circumstances. In every news broadcast of every major news outlet, the economy is center stage, and none of the news is good. Speculators are saying this downturn will last for years, and it's anybody's guess how to turn it around.

How quickly things have changed. If I had written this book just thirty months ago, the circumstances were exactly the opposite.

At that time, consumer spending was at an all time high among American households. Real estate values were skyrocketing across the nation. The stock market was strong; employment was good; and the outlook was bright and positive. Americans were making hundreds of thousands of dollars on their homes, buying second homes, cashing out to take vacations, and investing in innumerable pleasures and comforts in life.

Way back then—thirty months ago—anybody could get a loan and choose from a wide variety of options. Everybody was hiring. Interest rates were down, and investments were growing. The American economy had never been stronger.

And just thirty months later, we face the worst financial meltdown since before World War II. Daily we hear of automakers on the verge of bankruptcy, banks being bailed out, and investment bankers taking their lives out of desperation.

The shifting sands of financial stability have changed dramatically in a very short time. The economy may bounce back, but whether it is up or down, we should always live on *God's* economy.

Proverbs 23:4–5 teaches, *"Labour not to be rich: cease from thine own wisdom. Wilt thou set thine eyes upon that which is not? for riches certainly make themselves wings; they fly away as an eagle toward heaven."*

If you are living by the world's economic systems, then all of this news can be nothing less than depressing. What seemed so promising only months ago now seems so discouraging. What seemed quite secure and certain now seems quite risky and unpredictable.

I'm writing this book to introduce to you a better way. For there is a way to live above the economy—to live joyfully and peacefully regardless of your 401k status or what your home value has done in recent months. Whether the economy is weak or strong—whether you are employed or unemployed, there is a better way to navigate the economic challenges that we all face in life.

That better way is: Live on God's economy!

The economies of this world are shifting sand, but the truth of God's promises is a solid rock. In the coming days, you will either build your home and your hope upon the shifting sand of secular economics or upon the solid rock of God's unchanging promises. And in the coming pages, I hope to introduce you to those promises and principles—that you might establish your life and your future upon that which matters for all of eternity.

As a pastor of a growing Baptist church, I am passionate about helping people understand God's ways. His truth always stands, regardless of the politics or power struggles of our day. God's promises make us secure and His Word gives us an unchanging, steadfast foundation upon which to establish our lives. He will never fail you, and no economist or investment advisor can make you that promise!

Money is a sensitive subject to talk about—especially for a pastor. Even recently, the media has featured stories of financial impropriety and extravagance among some megachurch leaders. Needless to say, this raises all of our eyebrows! In addition, even Christians are sometimes extremely sensitive about a pastor speaking or writing on matters of biblical, financial stewardship.

I recently read about a woman who had a pet cat named Homer. She loved Homer very much, and when Homer unexpectedly died, she was very shaken.

She called a local Baptist church and asked the minister if he performed funerals for cats. Of course he said no and suggested she call the Presbyterian church—he thought that perhaps they conducted funerals for cats.

Well, of course the Presbyterian church didn't either and so they referred her to the Methodist church. The Methodist church passed as well. Finally she called the Baptist minister back being quite frustrated that no one would perform a funeral for Homer.

She said to the Baptist minister, "It's not like I'm asking for something for nothing! I'm more than willing to pay for the funeral. In fact, I was going to give a thousand dollars!"

Immediately, the pastor interrupted and said, "Well, why didn't you tell me that your dearly departed Homer was a Baptist? I would be happy to do the funeral!"

That humorous story reminds us all of the wrong extremes we've seen regarding organized religion and financial stewardship!

So why would I undertake such a risky endeavor—a pastor writing a book about financial stewardship? Because I desire God's best for your life! When we understand God's principles—God's economy—and submit ourselves to Him, He promises to meet all of our needs, not merely according to the need, but *according to his riches in glory by Christ Jesus"* (Philippians 4:19)!

These chapters will help you bring your financial decisions into the realm of God's blessing. That is not to say He will make you healthy and wealthy—but rather that He will honor those who honor Him. That's just the way He works (1 Samuel 2:30).

One of the reasons we have such a difficult time talking about money is that money is life transmuted into currency. Money is an expression of who we are and what we do. Money is simply taking the hours and the sweat and the work of our lives and translating it into a coinage that represents the passing of our days. Money is a naturalized citizen of every land and speaks all languages.

And God has much to say in His Word about money. There is no way that we could cover all of it in this small book, but I do ask of you a simple request. Read these chapters with an open heart. If you are sensitive about money issues—especially being talked about in church or by a pastor—set those sensitivities aside long enough to seriously consider God's Word and God's principles.

Long before I was a pastor, I became a Christian. Aside from being a pastor, I am a husband and father—a man who has needs, bills, and financial challenges and goals just as you do. I desire to care for my family, save carefully, invest wisely, and invest eternally as well. I desire to help my children get a good start in life, and I desire to help meet the needs of others around me.

In addition, for over twenty-five years I have watched two groups of Christians journey through their Christian lives—those who trust God's principles and those who do not. I can say from personal and pastoral experience that God's principles never fail. God honors those who honor Him! I have never seen Him fail to provide for those who live on His economy.

For those who refuse to trust Him, it seems they never really make it all work out on their own. And it never fails that they ultimately rob themselves of greater blessings and supernatural provision that God would have bestowed.

With these introductory thoughts, I would like to introduce you to God's economy. I would like to share ten principles—ten reasons that I trust God with my finances. In sharing, I challenge you to embrace these principles and to live them out for the rest of your life. As you align your life with God's promises, you will find peace, contentment, stability, security, and eternal benefit.

God says in Colossians 3:1–2, *"If ye then be risen with Christ, seek those things which are above, where Christ sitteth on the right hand of God. Set your affection on things above, not on things on the earth."*

Let's learn together how to set our affections on God's purposes. And after you set this book down, may you begin to experience the dramatic difference of living on God's economy!

CHAPTER ONE

Christ's Sacrifice Compels Me to Give

A friend of mine related an incident to me that occurred when he visited the Vietnam Veterans Memorial in Washington, D.C. He watched a man with tears streaming down his cheeks lovingly place a beautiful wreath at the base of the memorial.

My friend wondered who this man was remembering. Who had made such an impact that all these years later, he was still not forgotten? My friend put his hand on the man's shoulder to comfort him, and the man explained the reason for his tears, "Twenty-five years ago, my buddy stepped into the line of fire for me. The least I can do is say 'thanks.'"

Truly, when you are thankful for what someone has done for you, you desire to express your gratitude to that person. As great as the sacrifice of this young soldier was to die for his friend, a much greater sacrifice was willingly made for us two thousand years ago. Jesus was mocked, rejected, spat upon, beaten, and nailed to a cross for our sake—in our place.

Motivated by the Cross

Christian givers are motivated by the Cross. The more we reflect upon Christ's sacrifice for us, the more we will look for ways to express our gratitude to Him.

Amy Carmichael, an Irish missionary who spent fifty-five years pouring out her life in India in service to her Lord wrote, "You can give without loving, but you cannot love without giving." Paul wrote, *"For the love of Christ constraineth us…"* (2 Corinthians 5:14).

Very simply, increased love for Christ will equal an increased desire to honor Him through sacrificial giving. And this love for Christ comes through understanding Jesus' sacrifice for us.

What couldn't we give to the One who gave His very life for us? What would we ever want to withhold from the One who gave His all to us?

Great Love Equals Great Sacrifice

Scripture records the testimony of one woman whose great love for Christ resulted in great giving to Christ.

"And, behold, a woman in the city, which was a sinner, when she knew that Jesus sat at meat in the Pharisee's house,

brought an alabaster box of ointment, And stood at his feet behind him weeping, and began to wash his feet with tears, and did wipe them with the hairs of her head, and kissed his feet, and anointed them with the ointment."—LUKE 7:37–38

Scholars estimate the value of this ointment was equal to one year's wages. What prompted this costly gift? It was motivated by love—a grateful response to Christ's love for her.

Simon the Pharisee, in whose home this gift was given, condemned the woman for what he believed was a tremendous waste of resources. Simon illustrates the truth of the statement "a cold heart and a stingy hand often go together." Those who do not love Christ can never understand the love-motivated giving of God's people. When an unsaved person criticizes you for giving to the Lord's work, don't let it discourage you—he just doesn't understand how much God has given to you.

Christian givers are motivated by the Cross.

Christ answered Simon's criticism by identifying the woman's love and pointing out Simon's own lack of love: *"…she loved much: but to whom little is forgiven, the same loveth little"* (Luke 7:47).

It is only when we begin to comprehend our unworthiness of Christ's loving sacrifice for us that we respond in grateful love to Him. God's gift of salvation is so undeserved, so sacrificial, so unspeakably generous (2 Corinthians 9:15), that all who have experienced it are motivated to demonstrate their gratefulness in return.

God Measures Love and Sacrifice

It is that grateful love that matters the most to God. He does not measure the monetary value of our gifts, but the love-generated sacrificial value.

Jesus pointed his disciples to a poor widow to illustrate this truth. She entered the temple, following in the train of proud, wealthy men who no doubt sounded trumpets before them to announce their giving. After they ladened the offering receptacles with large tokens of their riches, she inconspicuously dropped in two mites, less than a penny in today's American currency.

Jesus gave us a glimpse into God's economy when He said, *"…this poor widow hath cast more in, than all they which have cast into the treasury"* (Mark 12:43). Obviously, God's accounting methods work differently from ours. We measure dollars and cents; God measures love and sacrifice.

To Jesus, the widow's mites were a greater gift than the rich men's wealth because *"all they did cast in of their abundance; but she of her want did cast in all that she had, even all her living"* (Mark 12:44).

This kind of complete sacrifice is the natural result of a Christian who meditates on Christ's sacrifice for him.

David Livingstone, a Scottish explorer and missionary to Africa, carried this desire to give to Christ, because he understood Christ's sacrifice for him. He wrote, "I place no value on anything I have or may possess, except in relation to the kingdom of God. If anything will advance the interests of the kingdom, it shall be given away or kept, only as by giving or keeping it I shall most promote the glory of Him to whom I owe all my hopes in time or eternity."

Biblical giving does not begin with money, but with surrender. God does not want our money as much as He wants what it represents—our hearts!

Willing Gifts Reflect a Willing Heart

Our love for God is reflected in the attitude with which we give. Some give to God like they are giving to the Internal Revenue Service, while others give like they are giving an engagement ring! The attitude makes all the difference, and, in light of Christ's sacrifice, the "engagement ring attitude" is the only option!

The story is told of a pastor who received a call on Sunday morning from the church pianist. She was sick and could not be in church. Hurriedly, the pastor asked another lady to play.

The would-be substitute was willing, but she only knew a few hymns. She listed them for the pastor, and he wrote them down for the congregational singing. Just before the service started, he asked her to have an additional song ready to play after he made the announcements.

The last announcement that morning was that the church needed to collect an offering to repair their roof due to recent storm damage. "Anyone who is willing to pledge to give $100 or more, please stand," the pastor requested.

Realizing this was the last announcement, the pianist took this as her cue to play. She began the only other song she knew—the national anthem! The entire congregation stood to their feet. Needless to say, that was the best offering this church ever received!

Unlike these church members who had no choice but to signify their pledged offerings, God desires that our gifts would be from the heart—a willing response to His sacrifice for us.

When the Lord directed Moses to collect an offering for the construction of the tabernacle, He instructed, *"Take ye from among you an offering unto the LORD: **whosoever is of a willing heart**, let him bring it…"* (Exodus 35:5). Six times in the account of this offering the word *willing* is used.

The response to Moses' invitation for willing givers was so great that those responsible for collecting the offering *"spake unto Moses, saying, The people bring much more than enough for the service of the work, which the LORD commanded to make. And Moses gave commandment, and they caused it to be proclaimed throughout the camp, saying, Let neither man nor woman make any more work for the offering of the sanctuary. So the people were restrained from* bringing. For the stuff they had was sufficient for all the work to make it, and too much" (Exodus 36:5–7).

God does not wrest money from us—He desires that we willingly give it in response to His great sacrifice for us. When we consider the sacrifice of Christ, we desire to give far more than what would normally be required or expected.

Another biblical example is seen years after the tabernacle was built, when King David collected supplies for his son Solomon to construct a more permanent place of worship, the temple. Again, people were given the opportunity to give, and they gave both willingly and generously: "Then the people rejoiced, for that they offered **willingly**…to the Lord…" (1 Chronicles 29:9).

> *When we consider the sacrifice of Christ, we desire to give far more.*

David encouraged this willingness to give by reminding the people, "…the work is great: for the palace is not for man, but for the LORD God" (1 Chronicles 29:1).

It is easy to give willingly when we meditate on the sacrifice Christ has made for us. We do not give primarily to the church or to others, but to the Lord. When we learn to look past the immediate recipient of our gifts to the Lord Himself, His sacrifice for us compels us to give freely and from the heart.

Consider where you would be if it were not for Christ's sacrifice, if His grace had not rescued you. Consider the many blessings you now enjoy because of what Christ has done for you—forgiveness of sins, a home in Heaven, promises of His provision, answered prayers, and many specific ways in which He has intervened in your life and in the lives of your family and loved ones.

Christ's loving sacrifice compels our action. Meditating on all He has done for us motivates our involvement in His economy.

CHAPTER TWO

The Example of First Century Christians Challenges Me to Give

Benjamin Broomhall, the secretary of the China Inland Mission, was invited to a friend's home for breakfast. The purpose of the breakfast was for the host and several other mutual friends to learn more about the missionary work in China.

In the course of the conversation, Mr. Broomhall read a letter he had recently received from a poor widow in Scotland who, out of her own poverty, regularly sent small sums of money for the work in China. "I can do without meat," the note read, "but the heathen in China cannot do without the Gospel."

One man present that morning said this dear lady's self-denial was "a shock to our personal self-indulgence." The host confessed that, while he had given large sums to the Lord's work over the years, he had never given sacrificially. As he expressed it, "it had not cost me a mutton chop."

This man pledged to give £500 ($34,000) to the work in China. Three others also gave similar amounts, and even a fourth man, who had been invited to that breakfast but could not attend, gave as a result of hearing this widow's story.

The sacrifice of other Christians is a tremendous challenge to our willingness to give. It challenges us to a greater spirit of sacrifice. It reminds us that poverty or wealth is not the dividing line of giving, but rather the willingness or unwillingness of each Christian's heart.

In God's economy, the motive is as important as the gift.

For example, Mississippi is the forty-ninth state in per capita income, yet it is the second highest state in per capita giving. Massachusetts is the fourth state in per capita income, yet it is the forty-ninth state in per capita giving.

As Warren Wiersbe wrote, "Christian giving does not depend on material circumstances so much as spiritual convictions."

Second Corinthians 8 describes the sacrificial offering of the poverty-stricken churches of Macedonia. Romans 15:26 explains that the purpose of this offering was *"to make a certain contribution for the poor saints which are at Jerusalem."* Very likely this poverty in Jerusalem occurred through persecution, and even though the Macedonian churches were poor themselves, they desired to give an offering to the Christians in Jerusalem.

Paul uses the example of these Christians' sacrifice to challenge the wealthy church at Corinth to step up to the plate in their giving.

"Moreover, brethren, we do you to wit of the grace of God bestowed on the churches of Macedonia; How that in a great trial of affliction the abundance of their joy and their deep poverty abounded unto the riches of their liberality. For to their power, I bear record, yea, and beyond their power they were willing of themselves; Praying us with much intreaty that we would receive the gift, and take upon us the fellowship of the ministering to the saints. And this they did, not as we hoped, but first gave their own selves to the Lord, and unto us by the will of God."
—2 Corinthians 8:1–5

Why is the testimony of these Macedonian Christians so powerful? The significance lies in their motive. In God's economy, the motive is as important as the gift. Some Christians give financially, but they give for the wrong reasons.

Early Christians Were Not Guilt-Givers

These Macedonian Christians did not give because Paul pushed or coerced them into giving. In fact, they had to beg

Paul to take their gift—*"Praying us with much intreaty that we would receive the gift…"* (2 Corinthians 8:4).

God never intended giving to hinge on guilt. He doesn't want you to give because you *have* to give, but rather because you *get* to give. When Christians give only so they will not feel guilty, they rob themselves of the joy of giving.

As a Christian, you will sense the Holy Spirit's conviction in your life if you do not obey His command to tithe or His prompting to give. This conviction is beneficial because it compels you to give according to God's plan for your finances. Submit and respond to this conviction—not just to be free of guilt, but to walk in obedience to the Lord.

Early Christians Were Not Greed-Givers

The Macedonian Christians did not give to get. They did not give because they hoped God would reward them with increased finances.

Some "health and wealth" teachers promise that if people give to their ministries, God will make these givers wealthy in return. This is not only an unbiblical teaching; it promotes an unscriptural motive.

God *does* load us with great blessings when we give. He gives far beyond our gifts to Him, as we will see more fully in chapter 7 of this book. Scripture is full of promises for givers. God even gives these promises to encourage us to give. In Malachi 3:10, He challenges us to give with the promise, *"Bring ye all the tithes into the storehouse, that there may be meat in mine house, and prove me now herewith, saith the LORD of hosts, if I will not open you the windows of heaven, and pour you out a blessing, that there shall not be room enough to receive it."*

When our basic motive for giving, however, is personal gain, we miss the bigger picture. Giving is not a game in which we have to try to trick God into increasing our blessings. God delights in blessing us; this is why He has promised to do so.

There is no need for greed in our giving. Rather, our motive should flow from an alternate purpose—grace.

Early Christians Were Grace-Givers

In Paul's account of the gift of these Macedonian Christians, he was careful to explain that biblical giving is the result of "the grace of God." The liberality of these Christian givers was not of themselves, but of God's grace bestowed on them.

Spiritual givers are motivated by grace; they give in response to God's work in their hearts. Grace is a disposition created in our hearts by God's Holy Spirit, and this was the motive behind these Macedonian Christians' gift.

Paul described grace in Philippians 2:13: *"For it is God which worketh in you both to will and to do of his good pleasure."* Grace is the powerful work of God in a Christian's heart to make him willing and able to do His will. Nothing short of grace-giving is biblical giving.

It was only through the grace of God that the churches of Macedonia gave so sacrificially out of their own deep poverty. As 2 Corinthians 8:3 explains, God's grace motivated these Christians to give *"beyond their power."* In other words, they gave more than they could or, from a human perspective, should.

Some Christians give *below* their ability; their gifts really cost them nothing. Some Christians give *at* their ability; they give what is available after they've budgeted other necessary expenditures. But other Christians, like these in the Macedonian churches, give *above* their ability; they give sacrificially, voluntarily setting aside "necessities" in their generosity.

> *Grace is a disposition created in our hearts by God's Holy Spirit.*

The grace-giving of the Macedonian Christians was the result of their giving first *themselves* to the Lord—*"but first gave their own selves to the Lord"* (2 Corinthians 8:5). Their financial giving followed as the natural by-product of this personal commitment, which we will examine more thoroughly in chapter 5 of this book.

Grace-giving surpasses the bounds of financial gifts. Hebrews 11:35–38 tells of many first century Christians who gave their bodies to be *"tortured…And others had trial of cruel mockings and scourgings, yea, moreover of bonds and imprisonment: They were stoned, they were sawn asunder, were tempted, were slain with the sword: they wandered about in sheepskins and goatskins; being destitute, afflicted, tormented; (Of whom the world was not worthy:) they wandered in deserts, and in mountains, and in dens and caves of the earth*"—all for the spread of the Gospel. This proves that they indeed gave of themselves before they gave their money.

Even in later centuries, our forefathers demonstrated grace-giving in giving of themselves. They gave with a depth of commitment that makes any financial gift I would give embarrassingly small in comparison. They loved God's work so supremely that they were willing to seal it in martyrs' blood.

I have visited the grave sites of men like William Tyndale (burned at the stake for translating the Bible into the English language), John Bunyan (imprisoned twelve years for preaching the Gospel), and many others.

These Christians left a legacy for us to follow. Their examples affirm the value of God's work and challenge us to give liberally and to invest our whole hearts.

Paul pointed the church at Corinth to the example of these generous Christians in Macedonia because he knew their godly example would motivate the Corinthian Christians to give. No doubt the Macedonian Christians were first challenged in their giving by the personal commitment of Paul. It was in Philippi (a city in Macedonia) that Paul's offering of himself was demonstrated through his willingness to endure a public whipping and dungeon imprisonment.

Paul's influence on the Macedonian Christians and the Macedonian Christians' influence on the Corinthian Christians, and all of their influences on us, should tell us something: if you want to be a generous person, associate with generous people.

There is something attractive about those who live with an open hand to God. Seeing them giving and receiving from God will challenge you to give more sacrificially.

God's economy operates on grace. When we consider the testimony of these first century believers (and many generations of others) who were poverty-stricken and often persecuted, their testimony challenges us to participate in grace-giving.

Guilt-giving and greed-giving ultimately produce resentment. But in grace-giving, you will find the joys of living on God's economy, which we will explore in our next chapter.

CHAPTER THREE

Jesus Instructs Me to Give

The story is told of a Christian businessman who approached his pastor after a sermon on tithing. "Pastor," he began, obviously uncomfortable, "that was a tremendous message, but, well, I really can't afford to tithe. I only make so much, and I have to support my family."

"Do you want to tithe?" the pastor asked.

"Of course I do, but I simply can't."

The pastor then made an offer to encourage this Christian businessman to put God first in his finances. "You begin tithing, but if you are ever short financially for meeting your family's needs, call me, and I will give you what you need."

The man was thrilled with such an offer! He could tithe, which he already knew he should be doing, but he didn't have to worry about failing to support his family. It was a win-win proposal.

Every week for a year, this businessman faithfully tithed, and surprisingly, he never had reason to call his pastor for financial help—all his needs were met. At the end of a year, he reflected on this experience. It was then that he realized he had been more willing to trust the promise of a man than the promises of God!

God commands us to give, but with this command is a multitude of promises that we will not lack. When we obey the command to give, we can be sure of God's provision for us.

Giving is not a minor topic in Scripture. In fact, the word *give* in its various forms is used 2,162 times throughout the Bible—that is more than *believe* (271 times), *prayer* (268 times), and *love* (714 times) all combined! Of the twenty-nine parables Jesus told, sixteen deal with money or possessions.

In addition to the parables on finances, Jesus preached on giving: *"Give, and it shall be given unto you; good measure, pressed down, and shaken together, and running over, shall men give into your bosom. For with the same measure that ye mete withal it shall be measured to you again"* (Luke 6:38). *"For where your treasure is, there will your heart be also"* (Matthew 6:21).

Yet, in spite of the vast material on giving, many Christians respond to even the mention of the word (and especially when coupled with the word *command*!) by reaching for their wallets—to hold them tightly closed.

Does this response reflect a true lack of resources? Can we really not afford to give? In these pages, you will see that the opposite is true—we can't afford *not* to give.

Giving Meets Our Needs

Even simple logic based on God's character tells us that God does not command us to do that which we cannot do. Thus, God's commands for giving do not rob us of our resources.

Why then, is our first reaction to giving often negative? It is because we do not understand, at least in our hearts, the true Source of our material provisions. Everything we have comes from God, and giving is an opportunity to remind ourselves of this truth.

God does not need our money, for He is the one who has given it to us! *"Every good gift and every perfect gift is from above, and cometh down from the Father of lights, with whom is no variableness, neither shadow of turning"* (James 1:17).

God does not command us to give to meet *His* needs—God has no needs. *"For every beast of the forest is mine, and the cattle upon a thousand hills. I know all the fowls of the mountains: and the wild beasts of the field are mine. If I were hungry, I would not tell thee: for the world is mine, and the fulness thereof"* (Psalm 50:10–12).

God commands us to give to meet *our* needs. More than we need any material goods, we need to know God as our Provider and Sustainer. Giving reminds us that everything we have comes from God, and it increases our awareness of our dependence on Him.

To meet our need to give, God has ordained a system in which He has voluntarily made His work dependent upon our giving. God could have set His work to perpetuate without monetary resources or to be supplied through other means than us, His people.

In God's economic system, however, we, the givers, are truly the recipients. When we give, God blesses us with far greater blessings than we yielded. (We'll examine these more thoroughly in chapter 7 of this book.)

In God's economic system, we, the givers, are truly the recipients.

Want proof that God's economy is primarily developed for our benefit and that God could do His work without our gifts? God's power is seen in His ability to multiply our gifts. He did this for the widow who gave of her meager meal to Elijah (1 Kings 17:10–15) and for the young boy who gave his lunch to Christ (John 6:9–12).

When we focus on the greatness of the financial needs in God's work, we lose the proper perspective. We compare the need to our resources and say, "My scanty resources won't even make a dent; it would be a waste for me to give." Instead, we should look at the greatness of our God to multiply even the smallest gifts of faith, and we should demonstrate that faith by obeying His command to give.

Giving Points Us to Our Provider

Giving frees us from the belief that we are our own providers. Even the man who has earned every penny he owns by the sweat of his brow must acknowledge Who gave him the job, the opportunity, the ability, the health to work.

As someone once commented, "The trouble with some self-made men is that they worship their creator." Giving to God is a tangible way of acknowledging that we are not self-made, that all we have comes from God.

Jesus told of a man who missed this truth to his own detriment.

"And he spake a parable unto them, saying, The ground of a certain rich man brought forth plentifully: And he thought within himself, saying, What shall I do, because I have no room where to bestow my fruits? And he said, This will I do: I will pull down my barns, and build greater; and there will I bestow all my fruits and my goods. And I will say to my soul, Soul, thou hast much goods laid up for many years; take thine ease, eat, drink, and be merry. But God said unto him, Thou fool, this night thy soul shall be required of thee: then whose shall those things be, which thou hast provided? So is he that layeth up treasure for himself, and is not rich toward God."
—LUKE 12:16–21

Notice how many personal pronouns this wealthy farmer used—a total of twelve, just in verses 17–19. For all the mentions of himself, he omitted references not only to God's provisions, but also to the hired servants or family who surely helped him plant, tend, and harvest this bountiful crop.

This farmer's pride gave him a false security. He wrongly translated God's prosperity into a misleading confidence in temporal wealth and abundance.

Because of our tendency to place our security in possessions, poverty is sometimes a greater blessing than prosperity. When we seek prosperity, we tend to lose our focus on Who has provided our blessings. Ecclesiastes 5:10 reminds us that wealth can never satisfy and warns of the folly of making money one's chief pursuit: *"He that loveth silver shall not be satisfied with silver; nor he that loveth abundance with increase: this is also vanity."*

Giving Teaches Us to Live by Faith

Biblical giving forces us to live by faith rather than by sight. The wealthy farmer that Jesus described looked at the intake from his harvest and determined what he would do for his future by what he saw.

Obedience to God's plan for giving forces us to live by faith, for faith is displayed by obedience. So just what does God command that we give?

The starting place for giving is found in Malachi 3:10, "*Bring ye all the tithes into the storehouse….*" Tithing is such an important command to God that He warns us we are literally robbing Him when we hold back the tithe. "*Will a man rob God? Yet ye have robbed me. But ye say, Wherein have we robbed thee? In tithes and offerings*" (Malachi 3:8).

God made an incredible promise to the nation of Israel when He said, "*Bring ye all the tithes into the storehouse, that there may be meat in mine house, and prove me now herewith, saith the Lord of hosts, if I will not open you the windows of heaven, and pour you out a blessing, that there shall not be room enough to receive it*" (Malachi 3:10).

Giving frees us from the belief that we are our own providers.

Although we are now living in the "church age" or the "age of grace," it is our conviction that a Christian would not give less under grace than the Old Testament saint did under the law.

Because God has prescribed a base proportion of ten percent, tithing is not truly *giving;* it is *bringing* God what already belongs to Him. Biblical giving begins when one gives above the tithe.

So many times, we try to rationalize ways to give less. One pastor told of a young man who asked him to pray for God's blessing on his career. At the time, he was making $40.00 per week and tithing $4.00. As he prayed with his pastor, he promised God that he would continue to tithe faithfully as God blessed him financially.

God honored this prayer, and before long, the young man was earning $5,000.00 per week. As this young man's income increased, his tithe check matched it, but his gratefulness did not. One day he returned to his pastor asking to be released from the promise to tithe. It was one thing to give $4.00 per week, but giving $500.00 weekly was more than he could bear.

The pastor agreed to pray with this young man about the situation. "Lord," he prayed, "this young man is having trouble tithing. Will you bring his income back down to $40.00 per week so he will be glad to tithe again?"

The young man stopped his pastor from finishing that prayer! "I understand, and I'm happy to tithe $500.00."

If there were no other reason to give, obedience would be a sufficient compelling factor. Yet God desires that we would not give out of obedience only, but also from hearts of love. When we thus give, we find the joy of living on God's economy.

CHAPTER FOUR

Giving Produces Joy

The story is told of a Christian carpenter during the Great Depression who loved the Lord and continued to faithfully give through his church, even during this economic crisis. When his church collected items to send to a missionary in China to meet his personal needs, as well as the needs of the orphanage he directed, the carpenter built the crates in which the donated articles would be sent. When the crates were full, the carpenter nailed them shut and readied them for shipment.

Later that evening, he reached into his pocket for his new glasses, but they were gone. He searched his entire shop for the missing glasses before he realized what must have happened—they had dropped from his pocket into one of the crates before he nailed it shut. His new glasses were now on their way to China. Initially, he was disappointed. The glasses were a special prescription and quite expensive.

Nothing could be done about it, however, so he simply began saving for new glasses.

A few years later, the missionary to whom the church sent the supplies visited the church of which the carpenter was a member during his furlough. "I want to thank you for the clothing and educational supplies you sent our orphanage," he began. "But, especially, I want to thank you for the glasses in the top of the last crate."

The church members looked at each other in surprise. They had not sent a pair of glasses—it wasn't even on their list of needed supplies.

"Just before your shipment arrived," the missionary continued, "my glasses were destroyed. Even if I had the money to replace them, it would be impossible in the city where I serve. Besides the difficulty of seeing without my glasses, I was experiencing severe headaches, so I was praying for the Lord to miraculously replace the glasses. When I opened your final crate and tried on those glasses, it was if they had been made perfectly for me—thank you."

Every church member in the congregation that evening assumed the missionary had confused their church with another—except for one, a hardworking carpenter sitting on the back row with tears of joy streaming down his face. Through his giving, God had allowed him to be part of a miracle.

Do you want to be happy? Really joyful? In God's economy, joy is the thrilling byproduct of giving. *"It is more blessed to give than to receive"* (Acts 20:35).

Willing Gifts Produce Joy

The greatest rejoicing in giving comes when we give willingly. We see this pattern throughout Scripture, but especially when the Israelites gave willingly for the construction of the temple: *"Then the people rejoiced, for that they offered willingly, because with perfect heart they offered willingly to the LORD: and David the king also rejoiced with great joy"* (1 Chronicles 29:9).

It is when we give from the heart that *we* most benefit from our gifts. Cheerful giving is rewarding, but grudging giving is discouraging to the giver. There are few things so burdensome to the heart as giving against your will.

> *It is when we give from the heart that **we** most benefit from our gifts.*

God Himself loves our cheerful gifts: *"Every man according as he purposeth in his heart, so let him give; not grudgingly, or of necessity: for God loveth a cheerful giver"* (2 Corinthians 9:7).

A mother who wanted to teach her daughter the joy of giving decided to let her learn experientially. Just before she and her daughter entered church, she gave the little girl a quarter and a dollar with the simple instructions, "Put one in the offering plate, and keep the other for yourself."

After the service, the mother asked her daughter which she had given—the quarter or the dollar. "I was going to give the dollar," the girl explained, "but just before the offering, the pastor reminded us to be cheerful givers. I knew I'd be a lot more cheerful if I gave the quarter, so I did."

While that humorous story may reflect the actions of some Christians, a mature Christian finds that he is more cheerful when he gives more and keeps less.

I thank the Lord for the incredible generosity of the Lancaster Baptist Church. By God's grace, our church family has given greatly to minister to our community and to develop a campus where people are ministered to and the next generation is trained for God's service. Our members have made sacrificial gifts of faith to build facilities for reaching our community and training students of West Coast Baptist College to reach other communities around the world. In our last missions conference, our members made a one year pledge of over one million dollars to support missionaries.

I've noticed that not only is our church a giving church; it is an incredibly happy church. This is because in God's economy, giving produces joy.

God has even physiologically designed our bodies to produce joy through giving. According to neuroscience researcher Jordan Grafman, brain scanning reveals that the joy of giving is "hard-wired into our brains."

The study monitored the brain activity of individuals playing a computer game in which they both received and donated money. The study found that the release of brain chemicals that trigger feelings of happiness and pleasure was greater when the participants were *giving* money than when they were *receiving* money. "It definitely seems like you're going to get more pleasure, if these brain activations can be any guide, when you're giving than when you're simply receiving," the researchers observed. (from the October 17, 2006 edition of the *Proceedings of the National Academy of Sciences*)

Giving Produces the Joy of Participation

One reason giving produces joy is because it provides opportunity for participation. *We* get to be a part of *God's* work!

God allowing us to participate in His work financially is similar to a father allowing his child to "go in on" a Mother's Day present. The father adds the child's quarter to his $50 gift. They give the gift together, and the child has the joy of participation.

Investing in God's work gives us a tangible means of laboring together with God in an eternal work. Then, when God blesses His work, we have the joy of knowing that we had a part.

Consider the young boy who gave his lunch to Jesus in Matthew 14. Jesus multiplied this gift and used it to feed over five thousand people! What a thrill it must have been for that boy to get to participate in this miracle.

Do you think Jesus took the boy's lunch because He needed it to feed the multitude? No, if He could multiply five small loaves and two fish into enough food to feed over five thousand people and have twelve baskets left over, surely he could have fed them without the lunch. He could have created food with His spoken word.

Yet, allowing this boy to donate his lunch gave the boy the incredible joy of knowing that he was a part. Can you imagine how much he enjoyed telling this story to his friends—and eventually his children and grandchildren?

You and I, too, get to have a part in God's work, and His economic system actually serves to our advantage. It works like this: God gives us everything we have. We invest a portion of it in His work. Then, God rewards us with blessings for giving what He first gave to us! What a tremendous economy system! We don't lose anything, and we gain so much.

David praised the Lord for the joy of being able to give what God first gave to him: *"Now therefore, our God, we thank thee, and praise thy glorious name. But who am I, and what is my people, that we should be able to offer so willingly after this sort? **for all things come of thee, and of thine own have we given thee**"* (1 Chronicles 29:13–14).

Giving Produces the Joy of Obedience

Aside from any other benefit of giving, there is a reward in obedience itself. Every time we respond to the Holy Spirit's promptings to give by faith, we grow in our relationship with the Lord. No amount of material wealth could substitute for this priceless treasure of a close relationship with the Lord.

When we refuse to give because we do not feel we have the resources, we forfeit opportunities to see God's supernatural provision. When we give and see God's provision, our faith is strengthened and we rejoice in God's blessings.

As God supernaturally provides for your needs, be sure to relay these stories to your children, your grandchildren, and any others you influence. They are faith-building and joy-producing for them, too!

A story I love to share with my children is of the Sunday morning my wife Terrie, baby daughter Danielle, and I were driving home from Indio, California, where I had preached that morning in the church I had started.

On Interstate 10, by Cabazon, California, our car broke down. Besides the frustration of

When we give and see God's provision, our faith is strengthened and we rejoice in God's blessings.

needing to get back home, we had no money to fix the car. We were in Bible college with very little money at the time, and even the gas to drive to Indio was a sacrifice.

We prayed for God to provide, and we waited in the car—with no air conditioning. The sweltering heat was almost unbearable. Terrie was sick, Danielle was fussy, and I was exhausted! We didn't know any mechanics in the area, and even if we did, we didn't have the money to pay them.

Before long, a middle-aged couple pulled up and stopped behind us. The man came up to our car. "What's the problem?" he asked. I told him what I knew about the situation, and he told us to get in the back seat of their Cadillac. "We'll take you to a mechanic."

We sank into the cool leather seats and reveled in the refreshing air conditioning. Terrie and I couldn't stop exchanging looks of amazement and wonder with one another. God was sure taking care of this need in style!

The couple drove us to a gas station just off the freeway and paid the mechanic there to tow and repair our car. The man then slipped a $100 bill into my hand and told us to have lunch in the restaurant that was next to the station while the car was being towed. We turned to thank them, and they were gone.

Terrie and I believe God sent angels "unawares" (Hebrews 13:2) to meet our need that day. Pastoring while attending Bible college may have been a strain both physically and financially, but it was well repaid by seeing the Lord meet our every need!

Giving Produces the Joy of Eternal Dividends

Giving produces the joy of making an eternal investment with eternal dividends. These investments can never be stolen or destroyed, for they are stored *"in heaven, where neither moth nor rust doth corrupt, and where thieves do not break through nor steal"* (Matthew 6:20).

No temporal investment can beat that! Cars rust, termites eat houses, companies go bankrupt, banks fail. We simply cannot keep what we invest here. We have no guarantee it will last. Proverbs 23:5 warns us of the brevity of temporal riches: "*Wilt thou set thine eyes upon that which is not? for riches certainly make themselves wings; they fly away as an eagle toward heaven.*"

Jim Elliot, a martyred missionary to Ecuador, had it right when he said, "He is no fool who gives what he cannot keep to gain what he cannot lose."

Christ has promised to every Christian "*an inheritance incorruptible, and undefiled, and that fadeth not away, reserved in heaven for you*" (1 Peter 1:4). We cannot buy our way to Heaven—Jesus already paid the price and offers it to us as a free gift. Neither can we take anything with us into Heaven. No wealth we amass on this earth can follow us into eternity. But we can choose to send riches ahead of us—the riches of eternal investments.

A humorous story about a very wealthy man who went to Heaven tells about his first sight of his heavenly dwelling. On the way, he passed many mansions of beauty and splendor.

Noticing a particularly magnificent home, he stopped the angel who was leading him. "Whose home is this?" he asked.

"Oh, that's Mr. Smith's home. You know him—he was your gardener on earth."

Impressed, the man continued walking. A few blocks later he stopped again, "Whose home is this?" he queried as he paused in front of a gorgeous, palace-like dwelling.

"This one," the angel answered, seeming happy to elaborate, "belongs to a missionary. She served the Lord many years. Your church supported her work."

Those who invest solely in this life lose on two counts—they miss the joys of giving here, and they miss the joy of eternal reaping.

The man blushed slightly when he remembered *he* had never given to this missionary's work, but he brightened quickly when he considered the prospects of his own heavenly mansion. If these were the homes of gardeners and missionaries, people who didn't have much money on earth, he could hardly begin to imagine the mansion he, the richest man in his county, would be given.

Soon the angel stopped in front of a small, one room, one window shack. The man had never seen such a dumpy place. "Whose house is this?" he asked aghast.

"Why, it's yours," the angel answered.

The man was shocked. "That can't be. The other homes were so beautiful. Why is mine so tiny?"

"I'm sorry," the angel replied. "We did all we could with what you sent us to work with."

While I don't believe there really are any such shacks in Heaven, this story reminds us that God has given us a choice between investing here or investing in eternity. In 1 Corinthians 3:11–14, He gives us the analogy of choosing what building material we want to use to build our lives. We can choose to build with that which is valuable and long lasting, or we can build with that which is easily destroyed and quickly decays.

Those who invest solely in this life lose on two counts— they miss the joys of giving here, and they miss the joy of eternal reaping.

Lee Iacoca, the legendary carmaker, wrote in his book *Talking Straight*: "Here I am in the twilight years of my life, still wondering what it's all about. I can tell you this: fame and fortune is for the birds." Resist the temptation of living for self; it's not worth the loss. Opt instead for the joys of making eternal investments.

Remember, however, that eternal investments only produce present joy if we maintain an eternal perspective. If we give grudgingly or for gain, we miss the joy of giving altogether. We must heed the admonition to *"Set your affection on things above, not on things on the earth"* (Colossians 3:2).

God's economy is vastly different from our world's economy—so totally opposite. In the world's economy, earning and hoarding wealth produces joy. In fact, most believe the more wealth one has, the happier he will be, when, in reality, nothing could be farther from the truth.

In God's economy, earning, saving, and sacrificing to give produces the greatest joy. The greater percentage in one's giving, the greater his joy in God's provision and his eternal dividends.

CHAPTER FIVE

My Commitment to Christ Calls Me to Give

King Frederick William III of Prussia was determined to free his country from Napoleon's rule. Men and boys throughout the country enthusiastically enlisted in the army. They, too, wanted to free the "motherland" from a hated yoke of oppression.

Lacking finances to fund what is now known as the Prussian War of Liberation, the king provided a way for the women to sacrifice for their country as well. He asked them to bring their gold and silver jewelry to be melted down for their country. In exchange, the women were given iron jewelry with the inscription *Gold gab ich für Eisen* ("I gave gold for iron").

The women donated their jewelry just as enthusiastically as the men had enlisted in the military. Wearing gold or silver jewelry became viewed as unpatriotic and the women prized their iron jewelry even more highly than the gold. It was proof that they had sacrificed for their king.

We, too, have the privilege to sacrifice for *our* King. When we remember His great sacrifice for us, we are moved to the sacrifice of true commitment.

Indicators of Commitment

To what are you really committed? Your car? house? education? career? Your commitment is revealed in the sacrifices you are willing to make. For instance, a committed deer hunter gladly rises at 3:00 AM to position himself in a tree stand before the twelve-point buck he hopes to harvest senses his presence.

Commitment and giving fit together—your giving is an expression of your commitment. Take a moment to evaluate your various financial commitments: housing, vehicle, entertainment, groceries, etc. Where does your giving fit into this list? And what does this reveal about your commitment to Christ?

Christ Deserves Total Commitment

Christ's sacrifice for us calls us to total commitment—a willingness to give anything and everything we have to Him.

A fear to give to the Lord exposes a lack of commitment. I'm amazed at Christians who hesitate to commit to weekly giving by saying, "I just don't know if I should make that commitment." Yes, commitment does have a cost, but a person who is committed is willing to pay whatever that price may be. All of us have *some* commitments. Perhaps you have signed a contract for your home or your vehicle. Doesn't Christ deserve an even greater level of commitment than is given through a contract?

Total commitment begins with offering ourselves. This is the pattern the Macedonian Christians followed: *"And this they did, not as we hoped, but first gave their own selves to the Lord, and unto us by the will of God"* (2 Corinthians 8:5).

Paul pointed out that such a commitment of one's self is only reasonable in light of what Christ has done for us. "*I beseech you therefore, brethren, by the mercies of God, that ye present your bodies a living sacrifice, holy, acceptable unto God, which is your reasonable service*" (Romans 12:1). Christ is worthy of our total commitment.

We Are Committed to Please Christ

By the strictest definitions, we don't really *give* anything to God; we only *manage* what He has entrusted to our care. The essence of life is not *ownership*; it is *stewardship*. As a steward, or manager, we have a responsibility to do with all God has entrusted to us exactly what He would do.

A committed Christian steward's highest priority is to please God, not himself. He does not see his finances as a tool to make himself wealthy or happy, but as a trust from the Lord.

To be a faithful steward who is committed to Christ, one must follow God's principles regarding finances. You cannot follow the world's philosophies of money and still manage it in a way that is pleasing to God.

Choose now to commit to making every financial decision based on God's Word. If you have not pre-determined to follow God's principles in this area, Satan will more likely be successful in using financial temptations to lure you away from your commitment to the Lord. For example, when your boss offers you extra hours if you will work every Sunday, you'll be more likely to accept the offer and be drawn away from faithful church attendance.

*The essence of life is not **ownership**; it is **stewardship**.*

This is why Jesus said, *"No man can serve two masters: for either he will hate the one, and love the other; or else he will hold to the one, and despise the other. Ye cannot serve God and mammon"* (Matthew 6:24).

The word *mammon* in this passage is a Syriac word which means riches or money. You will either *serve* Christ and *manage* your money, or you will serve *money* and be managed *by* the money. Your commitment to Christ makes the difference.

Each of us is a manager of a "trust." We are not free to spend the resources of the trust as we desire, we must remember we are only managers to disperse the resources according to God's ways.

The interesting thing about God's ways is that they are different from our ways; sometimes they are even the opposite. "*For my thoughts are not your thoughts, neither are your ways my ways, saith the LORD*" (Isaiah 55:8).

Our ways to manage and increase money would include borrowing, working harder, saving more, etc. While there is certainly a place for these practices, God tells us the primary way He wants us to invest and increase His money. He says, "*Give, and it shall be given unto you…*" (Luke 6:38).

What? The primary way to increase our finances is to give them away? Remember, His ways are different—higher and better—than our ways. We simply must be committed to following them.

God Promises to Bless Commitment

At the time of this writing, over eight hundred *thousand* Americans have lost their homes through foreclosure in the past few months alone. Many of the contracts signed for these homes were deceptive, in that lenders allowed young couples to qualify for loans they could never afford.

God's call to commitment is refreshing in that it carries none of this deception; rather, it carries guaranteed success. To those who are committed to follow His way of tithing, He says, "*…prove me now herewith, saith the LORD of hosts, if I will not open you the windows of heaven, and pour you* *out a blessing, that there shall not be room enough to receive it"* (Malachi 3:10). God positively promises to bless those who follow His principles with their finances.

Not long after our family arrived in Lancaster, we experienced a particularly difficult week of financial need. We were literally wondering how we would buy groceries for the coming week. Our cupboards were bare, our checking account depleted, and our commitment was being tested.

That Sunday evening, a couple of families in the church invited us to join them for a bite to eat at a local fast food taco restaurant called Naugle's. The invitation was a blessing because we didn't have food at home that we could prepare.

That evening, we were the last ones to leave the church after locking up. As we drove to the restaurant, it occurred to me that our hosts were probably already eating, which meant we would most likely need to pay for our own dinner. As we drove, I asked Terrie to give me some money. She said, "I don't have any money."

Now, usually when a wife says she doesn't have any money, she still has some! So I said, "I know you don't, but give me some money so I can pay for dinner."

My wife looked at me with big tears in her eyes and said, "Paul, not only do I not have any money, but we don't even have any food at home, and I'm not sure what we're going to eat tomorrow."

I cannot describe to you how I felt in that moment. While I knew we were following God to Lancaster, I felt that

I had failed as a provider. Immediately, I turned to human solutions. I asked our five-year-old daughter Danielle to look under the seats for any spare change. A few moments later she had managed to find a grand total of seventy-two cents. With disappointment I decided this was enough to buy an iced tea for the whole family to share, and we would tell our hosts that "we just weren't hungry."

It was about that time that Terrie looked at me and asked the obvious, "Why don't we pray about it?" A little embarrassed that *I* hadn't thought of this, I swallowed my pride and began to explain our situation to the Lord and ask for His provision.

Moments later, we stepped into Naugle's, and before we could even begin to order our iced tea, the cashier held up two large bags of food and said, "Sir, we just had a van full of teenagers come by the drive-through, order all this food, and then drive off. Would you like to eat it?"

Grace-givers continually ask, "How much can I give?"

Terrie and I looked at each other with tears in our eyes. We high-fived, hugged, and rejoiced in God's provision. We returned home with full stomachs to bare cupboards, but we had confidence that God would come through.

At 7:00 the next morning, there was a knock on our door. I was surprised to see dear friends, Pastor Rick Houk and his wife, standing at our door with their arms full of grocery bags. He said, "Brother Chappell, the Lord put you and your family on our hearts last night. Our church took an offering; we went to a twenty-four hour grocery store, and we drove straight here through the night to deliver these groceries!"

We were reminded once again that truly our Heavenly Father is a faithful provider! This was only the first of many times over the years that God has wonderfully provided for our every need.

God can be proven; His ways are trustworthy. It is safe to commit yourself to the Lord.

Commitment Is Fueled by Grace

What fuels this commitment to Christ? What keeps the wise steward motivated to give? It is nothing less than the grace of God, for giving is a grace.

Legalistic methods of giving focus on how *little* one can give and still meet God's basic requirements and enjoy His generous blessings. Grace-givers, however, continually ask, "How *much* can I give?"

I once saw a bumper sticker in North Carolina that addressed commitment in giving. It read, "Tithe if you love Jesus, any idiot can honk." There is no such thing as a committed Christian who is not also a giving Christian.

As Christians increase in maturity, they increase in sacrificial giving. Paul reminded the Corinthian church that just as they grew spiritually in other areas of their lives by grace, they could grow in their giving through grace as well.

*"Therefore, as ye abound in every thing, in faith, and utterance, and knowledge, and in all diligence, and in your love to us, see that ye **abound in this grace** also"* (2 Corinthians 8:7).

He reminded them that Jesus was the example of this grace: *"For ye know the grace of our Lord Jesus Christ, that, though he was rich, yet for your sakes he became poor, that ye through his poverty might be rich"* (2 Corinthians 8:9).

It was this very grace of Christ that calls us to participate in His economy. As Paul explained to these Christians, giving to the Lord was a way to *"prove the sincerity of your love"* (2 Corinthians 8:8). Truly, our willingness to live on God's economy, first by giving ourselves, and then by giving our finances, is a reflection on our commitment to Christ. The committed Christian is a giving Christian.

CHAPTER SIX

The Mission of My Church Is Worthy of My Investment

I heard a story of a conversation between Joe, an American on a missions trip to China, and Yongni, a Chinese national.

"What will be the first thing you do when you get to Heaven?" Joe asked.

"That's easy," Yongni answered. "I'll look for Jesus and thank Him for giving His life for me so I can be in Heaven."

"Well, of course, you would do that first, but what will you do next?"

"After I thank Jesus, I'll find the missionary who told me about Jesus. I'll thank him for leaving his home country and his family and friends and coming to a strange culture to tell me the good news of the Gospel."

"Then what will you do?" pressed Joe, a little impatiently.

Without a moment's hesitation, Yongni replied, "I will find every person who ever gave to support that missionary—every man who gave his hard-earned money, every child who emptied his piggy bank, every widow who sacrificially went without, every Christian in every church who gave in any way to support the missionary who brought me the Gospel. I will search all of Heaven until I find every one of them."

When I heard this story, it made me ask myself, "Who in Heaven will be looking for me? Who will be my eternal friend in Heaven because of my giving on this earth?"

The Value of the Local Church

Is there a work on earth that Christ considers His? Is there a work on earth that Christ considers worthy of sacrifice? Jesus' example answers both of these questions with a resounding "YES!"

This work is the local church, and Jesus loved the church so much that He purchased it with His own blood. Ephesians 5:25 explains, "...*Christ also loved the church, and gave himself for it.*"

I love the local church! I praise the Lord for the opportunity to have been raised in church. God used my many Sunday school teachers, each sermon I heard, the church camps I attended—every aspect of the church to influence and shape my life. Even as a child, He used the local church to give me a desire to live with eternal values.

Today, I'm thankful for the love and fellowship of my church family. I'm thankful to Him that I could be part of something so awesome, so needed, so eternal as the local church.

Do you love your church? In what ways has the local church impacted your life? Thank God for the many ways the local church has benefited you—salvation, spiritual growth, opportunities for service, help in directing your children's hearts to God—the list is long.

The Mission of the Local Church

There is no greater investment you can make than that of helping others to hear of Christ and spend eternity in Heaven. There is no possession, no status, no accomplishment that is even comparable to investing in the souls of men.

The mission of the local church is worthy of our investment. Christ gave the local church the responsibility of reaching the entire world with the Gospel: "…*ye shall be witnesses unto me both in Jerusalem, and in all Judaea, and in Samaria, and unto the uttermost part of the earth*" (Acts 1:8).

Your church has the responsibility of reaching every person in the community with the Gospel of Christ. Christ has commanded His church to "*Go out into the highways and hedges, and compel them to come in, that my house may be filled*" (Luke 14:23). What a joy to get to be part of such an awesome responsibility!

But the mission of your church doesn't end in your community. Christ also commanded the church to "*Go ye into all the world, and preach the gospel to every creature*" (Mark 16:15). Five times in Scripture this command to reach the entire world is given. We call it the Great Commission.

Fulfilling the Great Commission, both in your community and around the world, does not hinge primarily on finances. It requires the power of the Holy Spirit working through each Christian's yielded life. Only the Holy Spirit can convict the lost of their sin and of their need to trust Christ. Only the Holy Spirit can use us—sinners saved by grace—to make known the wonderful salvation He freely offers.

> *When you give **to** your church, you literally are giving **through** your church.*

But the work of God on Earth cannot happen without resources, and God has chosen to bless His people that they might sustain His work. This gives us the incredible opportunity to be a part of lives being changed through the power of the Gospel. We get to invest in the greatest financial investment of all time!

When you give *to* your church, you literally are giving *through* your church. The money you give to your church goes to supporting your pastor (see 1 Timothy 5:17–18 and 1 Corinthians 9:14) as well as providing for the local ministries of your church. It also goes to support the work of missionaries around the world. The money you give has worldwide eternal impact—what a worthy investment!

Giving Will Grow Your Love for Your Church

Even in the Old Testament, God gave His people the opportunity to invest financially in worshiping Him. When He delivered them from slavery in Egypt, He miraculously parted the Red Sea, but when it came time to build the Tabernacle in the wilderness, He did not miraculously create it. He wanted His people to invest in this project, because He knew that when they invested their money, they would also invest their hearts.

Sometimes people ask me how they can develop a greater love for the work of the Lord in their church as well as on mission fields around the world. I always give them the same answer—give more, *"For where your treasure is, there will your heart be also"* (Luke 12:34).

> *When we invest our money, we also invest our hearts.*

David was a man who modeled this love for the Lord in his giving. Shortly before he died, he collected an offering for the construction of a magnificent temple his son, Solomon, was to build. He himself gave 110 *tons* of gold! This gift is particularly revealing of David's heart of love for God when one considers that he was giving toward something that he would not see in his lifetime.

Give to Impact Eternity

I thank God that the people of Lancaster Baptist Church have been willing to freely and generously invest in the Lord's work through our church. The first stewardship event at our church was in 1988, and we used the theme "Giving by Faith." Our church was growing rapidly, and we knew we needed property and a new building.

A small group of families sacrificially gave $50,000. In so doing, they demonstrated their love for the work of the church.

This money was used as the down payment for the seventy-eight acre property our church now owns. Over the years, our church has continued to invest in the Lord's work here at Lancaster Baptist. God has blessed our giving and provided us with a beautiful campus for ministry.

Frequently, I leave my office to walk around the campus and thank God for the ministry that takes place here. On a recent Saturday, I saw our ball field full of boys practicing with the church baseball league and learning from the godly men coaching them; in our auditorium there was a wedding of two young people who had grown up in our church; in the office building were young couples receiving premarital counseling; in every building, people were setting up for Sunday classes and ministries. Each of these facilities and the opportunities they provide for investing in people's lives all began with a young church that was willing to invest in God's work.

Perhaps your church is smaller in size, but even so, its ministry has just as much eternal impact on each person it reaches. When you give through your church, you get to have a part in people being saved, lives being changed, and young people being trained for lifelong obedience to God. One person said it this way: "Use your affluence for eternal influence."

When one pastor told his church of the need for new Sunday school buildings, a lady came to him after the service and said, "I'm glad you said you didn't know who was going to help pay for the new Sunday school buildings; for a minute there, I thought you were going to ask us!"

She had it all backwards—it was an opportunity, not a burden. Thank God for every member of every church who gives for the cause of Christ.

Giving to charities and non-profit causes may be appropriate and helpful at times. Remember, however, that the local church is the institution that was given the Great Commission, and giving through the church is the best way to see eternal fruit for your giving. The church is capable of providing much more than humanitarian aid; it brings people spiritual truth—God's simple plan of salvation. Jesus Himself gave His life for the church.

Investing in the ministry of the local church is the greatest investment you could ever make. It is both a worthy and rewarding investment with eternal dividends.

I love the humorous story of Sam and Bob—two men who were stranded on a deserted island after a shipwreck. With no food or potable water on the island, their future looked pretty bleak.

Sam began pacing the beach wringing his hands in desperation. "We're going to die, we're going to die," he repeated over and over. Seeing Bob sitting against a tree calmly watching the tide come in didn't help his disposition.

"Don't you understand?" he screamed at Bob. "We're going to die!"

"No," Bob replied, "we'll be all right. I make $100,000 a week."

"What difference does that make now?" Sam chided. "Even if we had all the money in the world, there are no stores here."

"You don't understand," Bob explained. "I make $100,000 each week, and I tithe. My pastor will find me!"

Giving to his local church was a good thing for Bob! But there are much greater reasons to give. In God's economy, the local church is the ultimate investment firm. Its mission is worthy of your investment. In exchange for financial gifts, you get to be a part of bringing people to Heaven. There is no greater use of your money.

In addition, God returns your investment with both temporal and eternal blessings—which is the subject of our next chapter.

CHAPTER SEVEN

Giving Positions Me for God's Blessings

A pastor in Glaucha, Germany, by the name of August H. Francke was concerned for the many orphans and street children in his town. In 1695, he began a one-room school to provide free education for these children. Soon, he expanded his ministry to a full orphanage, and by 1698, he had over one hundred orphans in his care.

Francke was far from wealthy, and the orphanage was supported mainly by Christians who followed the principle of James 1:27 and gave sacrificially: *"Pure religion and undefiled before God and the Father is this, To visit the fatherless and widows in their affliction…."*

One afternoon, Francke heard a knock at his door and opened to find a poor widow in great financial need. Francke himself was lacking needed funds for the orphans, but he sensed the Holy Spirit moving him to give this dear widow a ducat (an old European gold coin)—his last coin. He gave his coin to the widow, trusting the needs of the orphanage to the Lord.

A couple of days later, Francke received a letter from this widow. She thanked him for the money and explained that she had prayed for God to bless the orphanage for his sacrifice. That very day, fourteen more ducats were sent to the orphanage—twelve from a wealthy woman in Germany and two from a friend in Sweden.

And the windows of Heaven hadn't closed yet! Soon news came that the orphanage would be receiving *five hundred* ducats from the estate of Prince Lodewyk Van Wurtenburg! When Francke sacrificially provided for the widow in need, he had been enriched, not impoverished.

One of the most unusual paradoxes is found in Proverbs 11:24, *"There is that scattereth, and yet increaseth; and there is that withholdeth more that is meet, but it tendeth to poverty."* How could scattering what one has increase his possessions? Why would saving what one has bring poverty?

In God's economy, giving is like planting a seed.

This verse portrays a farmer planting his seed. If he scatters his seed into the ground, apparently losing its value for his personal use, it multiplies; but if he hoards it in his barn, apparently preserving it to meet his own needs, he has no increase and will eventually go hungry.

In God's economy, giving is like planting a seed. Just as planting seed positions a farmer for harvest, so giving our resources positions us for God's blessings. Second Corinthians 9:6 explains it this way, "...*He which soweth sparingly shall reap also sparingly; and he which soweth bountifully shall reap also bountifully.*"

Jesus also explained the direct relation between giving and blessing in Luke 6:38: "*Give, and it shall be given unto you; good measure, pressed down, and shaken together, and running over, shall men give into your bosom. For with the same measure that ye mete withal it shall be measured to you again.*" This verse reminds us that giving follows four basic laws of harvest.

You Reap What You Sow

"*Give, and it shall be given unto you...*"

You simply cannot out-give God! And every Christian who has been giving to God long enough to reap the harvest can attest to this truth.

Prior to our move to Lancaster, my wife and I had saved several thousand dollars in hopes that someday the Lord would allow us to purchase a home. But coming to Lancaster required that we put all that money into moving, renovating the church, and starting the ministry. So we were back to square one when it came to saving for a home—and we were taking a church that offered no salary.

Our housing options then were very limited—so limited that when my wife first saw the small duplex in which we would be living, she cried! It was quite dilapidated and had no air conditioning (this was August in California) and no working stove.

Even so, we were thankful for a place to live, and we adjusted to the inconveniences and threw our energies into building the church.

Not long after, some long-time friends we hadn't seen in a while came to visit. The weather was extremely hot that day, and walking into our home was like walking into a sauna. On top of that, we lived in a very bad part of town— the kind of place where no one really wants to spend a lot of time.

For this reason, we weren't surprised when our guests immediately suggested we all take a drive and see the area. The car had great air conditioning which made their idea all the more attractive!

As we were driving, we passed by a new home development with a sign that said, "Only One House Left." Suddenly, our friend turned the car and said he wanted to take a look at that house. We assumed he was interested in possibly making an investment purchase.

A few moments later, we had walked through the three bedroom house, and our friend began talking to the real estate agent. He asked how much money was needed for a down payment on the house. We were hoping he would buy the house and then allow us to rent it from him.

When the agent told us the amount, it was the exact amount we had depleted from our savings when we moved to Lancaster. In that moment, our friend took out his checkbook and gave the agent the down payment.

I cannot describe to you the joy and emotion that filled our hearts that day when our friends told the agent that this home would be in our name and that the down payment was their gift to us. We were amazed and grateful.

The story doesn't end there! Our friend arranged for us to live in the house immediately and negotiated a deal for us to live in the house payment free until escrow closed.

The best part about this story to me is that it is just one of many. I could literally fill the rest of this book, and several more besides, describing how God has blessed our giving with His favor.

Experiencing God's blessing after giving is not a privilege given only to a select few. It is a basic law of God's economy—you will always reap what you sow. The shape and size of the harvest will vary from one experience to the next, but the blessings will always come.

You Reap More Than You Sow

"… *good measure, pressed down, and shaken together, and running over, shall men give into your bosom*…."

One of the outstanding characteristics of God's economy is the generosity of God. He gives far more than what we give to Him.

God has built multiplication into the laws of harvest. For example, one wheat seed can produce over one hundred more seeds on one plant, and one corn seed may produce a stalk with over eight hundred kernels per ear.

God blesses our giving with this same multiplication. One generous Christian observed, "I shovel out, He shovels in, and He has a bigger shovel!" This could be the personal testimony of hundreds of thousands of Christians who have chosen to live on God's economy—God richly rewards those who give. *"The liberal soul shall be made fat: and he that watereth shall be watered also himself"* (Proverbs 11:25).

God's rewards are not limited to monetary blessings. Christians who give find that God's blessings include the joy of being used, increased dependence upon Him, growth in faith, contentment, and even eternal rewards.

Remember, however, that to reap more than you sow, you must be willing to plant the seed. *"Verily, verily, I say unto you, Except a corn of wheat fall into the ground and die, it abideth alone: but if it die, it bringeth forth much fruit"* (John 12:24). Harvest reaping always follows spring planting. In other words, the process starts when you give.

You Reap in Proportion as You Sow

"…For with the same measure that ye mete…"

Every spring our family plants a garden in raised beds in the backyard. One year, I decided to plant pumpkins. Not familiar with how profusely they produce and spread,

I planted lots of pumpkins. We had so many pumpkins, our entire backyard became a pumpkin patch, and all the children in our church were able to come out and pick one.

If I plant pumpkins now, I don't plant nearly as many. I do plant plenty of tomatoes, however, because my wife loves tomatoes—fresh and canned. I plant in proportion to the harvest I desire.

We should remember this principle in our giving, too—God's blessings are in direct proportion to our giving. In fact, in God's economy, giving is a form of investing. J.L. Kraft, founder of Kraft Cheese, regularly invested twenty-five percent of his income in the Lord's work. Later he observed, "The only investment I ever made which has paid consistently increasing dividends is the money I have given to the Lord."

Investing wisely and giving generously are not opposing concepts; they are complementing truths. Proverbs 19:17 says, *"He that hath pity upon the poor lendeth unto the LORD; and that which he hath given will he pay him again."*

If we only knew how richly God would bless

Investing wisely and giving generously are complimenting truths.

our giving, we would not even be tempted to withhold anything from Him! Oswald Chambers reminded us to give generously when he said, "It is not how much we give, but what we do not give that is the real test."

You Reap After You Sow

"…it shall be measured to you again."

I've never known a farmer to plant his field and then be disappointed the next morning when there is no harvest. We all understand the results of planting are not immediate. And so it is with giving—the blessings are guaranteed, but they are not immediate.

Some of our reaping will not come until we see the fruit of our eternal investments in eternity. Some of our reaping will come sooner. But either way, it will come. God has promised, *"…it **shall** be measured to you again."*

Giving involves faith. You must believe that if you give, sometimes even of that which you yourself need, God will bless you. God's Word is full of promises to sustain such faith:

"Blessed is he that considereth the poor: the LORD will deliver him in time of trouble."—Psalm 41:1

"He that hath a bountiful eye shall be blessed; for he giveth of his bread to the poor."—Proverbs 22:9

"He that giveth unto the poor shall not lack: but he that hideth his eyes shall have many a curse."—Proverbs 28:27

"Bring ye all the tithes into the storehouse, that there may be meat in mine house, and prove me now herewith, saith the LORD of hosts, if I will not open you the windows of heaven,

and pour you out a blessing, that there shall not be room enough to receive it."—Malachi 3:10

"*And God is able to make all grace abound toward you; that ye, always having all sufficiency in all things, may abound to every good work:*"—2 Corinthians 9:8

"*But my God shall supply all your need according to his riches in glory by Christ Jesus.*"—Philippians 4:19

One of the greatest enemies of giving is worry—we fear that if we give, we really won't have enough. Worry, however, is a fruitless expenditure of strength and a definite deterrent of faith. As one person said, "Worry pulls tomorrow's cloud over today's sunshine."

An exasperated husband once asked his wife, "Why are you always worrying when it doesn't do any good?" She quickly piped back, "Oh, yes it does! Ninety percent of the things I worry about never happen." She had the right answer with the wrong conclusion!

George Müller wrote, "The beginning of anxiety is the end of faith, and the beginning of true faith is the end of anxiety." Instead of worrying, trust God's promises to provide and His principles of harvest.

Giving is a form of planting—and reaping. It positions you directly under the windows of Heaven, available to receive the lavish blessings of God.

Can you imagine the blessings God could pour on your life if you were positioned under the windows of Heaven to receive it? In God's economy, the blessings we receive are far greater than anything we give to the Lord.

CHAPTER EIGHT

My Children Will Follow My Example

In San Jose, California, where my wife Terrie and I both grew up, a local newspaper sponsored an annual treasure hunt. The newspaper staff would hide a little tube somewhere in the Silicon Valley, and each day they would publish a clue leading to its location on the front page of the paper. The first person to find the tube won a cash prize!

One year, Terrie and her mom decided to hunt for this treasure. They diligently searched the San Jose countryside every day. They spent many hours that summer looking for the mysterious tube. When the tube was finally found and the discovery published in the paper, they learned that for all the time and effort they had exerted, they never even came close to finding it.

Many of us spend our lives looking for things of no eternal value like that hidden tube. Perhaps your "tube" is popularity, wealth, or success in your career—things that are not necessarily wrong, but that should be secondary to eternal investments.

The saddest result of such actions is that our children observe this empty search, but they are too immature to discern its fruitless results; thus they repeat it, and the cycle continues through the generations.

On the other hand, when you demonstrate the pursuit of eternal values to your children, you encourage them by your example that treasure is to be stored in Heaven's bank and that God promises eternal rewards for sacrificial giving.

Recognize the Weight of Your Influence

Someone once said, "Don't worry that your children never listen to you; worry that they are always watching you." Every parent has learned just how true this is! Our children watch us very closely, and they take our actions for their pattern.

The desire in children to be like their parents is so strong that many times they will imitate their parents' actions without even understanding the significance behind the actions.

One little boy whose dad worked long, hard hours in construction admired everything about his dad. When the dad returned home tired from a long day of work one evening to find his son purposefully covering himself—from head to foot—in mud, he sternly told him to go inside and wash up. "But, Dad," the little boy answered, "I want to be just like you!" This little one admired his dad so much that he attempted to imitate everything his dad did.

One young wife was observed cutting off the ends of a ham before placing it in the pan to bake. When asked why she removed the ends, she explained, "I don't know; that's just the way my mother always did it." Later she asked her mother about it and learned that *her* mother did the same. When the young wife and her mother questioned the grandmother, they learned the secret. "That was the only way I could make the ham fit in my pan!"

Your influence carries tremendous weight—invest it in your children by modeling participation in God's economy.

Display Eternal Values

Values are more accurately "caught than taught." Regardless of what you say, your children will be far more likely to define their values by your actions than by your words. This is why it is vital that your actions point your children to eternal, rather than temporal values.

Your children themselves are eternal treasures, loaned to you by the Lord to train for Him. Demonstrate wise stewardship by investing in your children. Spend time with them, train them, play with them.

Some parents neglect their children by making their careers a higher priority than their families. Children are sensitive, however, and see the value implications of these choices. Remember that no mansion or limousine can even begin to compare in value to the worth of your children. Treasure your family by guarding your heart against unbalanced pursuit of material blessings.

Every loving parent desires to provide the very best for his child. God gave you this desire to give to your children. As a Father, God Himself gives to us. *"Every good gift and every perfect gift is from above, and cometh down from the Father of lights, with whom is no variableness, neither shadow of turning"* (James 1:17).

Invest in your children by modeling participation in God's economy.

It is not temporal blessings themselves that are dangerous. God Himself provides these blessings. The danger for our children comes when they observe us pursuing these blessings with distorted values.

Our children need to see the purpose for which God provides *"us richly all things to enjoy"* (1 Timothy 6:17). It is that we may *"do good…be rich in good works, ready to distribute, willing to communicate"* (1 Timothy 6:18). In other words, God gives us blessings that we may give to others.

Develop appetites in your children for eternal values by modeling and allowing them to participate in giving to the Lord's work.

Teach Biblical Financial Principles

While your *values* will be better caught than taught, the "how to" of living out those values will need to be taught. God's economy operates on the wisest and best financial principles. These are all found in God's Word and proven in the lives of all who sincerely try them. God has entrusted parents with the responsibility of training their children in the ways of God: *"And thou shalt teach them diligently unto thy children…"* (Deuteronomy 6:7).

A sometimes overlooked principle when teaching children is that of tithing. After all, is it really necessary for them to tithe? What difference does a child's dime make in the church's budget anyway? It may not make a significant difference in the church's finances, but it does make a difference in the heart of your child. Tithing reminds all of us that everything we have comes from God.

Because children have tender hearts, they *delight* in giving to the Lord. By teaching them to tithe ten cents when they are six, their heart will remain tender, and it will be much easier for them to tithe twenty dollars when they are sixteen.

In God's economy, hard work, thrifty living, purposeful, systematic saving, and wise investing are all important. And all of these principles are taught in God's Word.

No parent wants his child to be financially unstable. We all want our children to be prepared for life's financial responsibilities.

One prospective father-in-law asked his daughter's boyfriend, "How much money do you have in the bank?"

"I don't know," replied the young man, "I haven't shaken it lately."

This young man needed more teaching in biblical financial principles!

As you prepare your children for financial stability, be sure to teach them in the context and from the perspective of living on God's economy. Saving and investing should enhance giving—not take away from it.

Leave a Legacy of Grace

Parents desire to leave an inheritance and a legacy for their children. Proverbs 13:22 says, *"A good man leaveth an inheritance to his children's children...."* A wise parent will plan ahead for his children and even his grandchildren.

If you can leave your children with resources that you know will be wisely invested in God's economy, that is wonderful. Remember, however, that temporal resources are only temporal. If you leave your children with God's principles deeply ingrained in their hearts through your example and teaching, you will leave an even greater inheritance than financial resources. You will have taught your children to be positioned for dividends in God's economy.

Inheritances have the unique potential of damaging family relationships when the family members do not understand eternal values. In twenty-four years of pastoring, I've seen many families torn apart over inheritance conflicts.

I will l never forget one of my first funerals I conducted in Lancaster. The lady who died was one of our church members who had been saved in her seventies—about six years before God called her home. When I went out to the back at the funeral to shake hands with her family, I walked into an unbelievable scene. Her children were screaming at each other, claiming what each felt to be his rightful portion of what she had left behind. I had to step in between forty and fifty-year-old "children" to stop them from fighting at their mother's funeral!

Truly, teaching your children to live on God's economy is the best legacy you can leave.

A young businessman in New York City was waiting for the subway. He had mistakenly left his watch at home, so he asked a man nearby what time it was.

"In which country?" the man asked.

"Do you have all the time zones on your watch?"

"This watch has all the time zones for each state in the U.S. and every country in the world. It is also GPS-enabled, can send faxes, email, and even pick up satellite television signals and display them on a miniaturized LCD color-pixilated screen!"

Clearly impressed, the young businessman asked the watch owner where he could buy such a watch.

"To tell you the truth, I'm getting bored with mine. I bought it for $2,000, but I'll just sell it to you for $900."

The young businessman whipped out his checkbook and bought the watch on the spot.

The previous watch owner handed over the watch and walked away, leaving his two suitcases.

"Wait," the young businessman called out, "you forgot your suitcases."

"Those," replied the watch man, "are the batteries."

Parents all across America fill their children's lives with expensive "fluff," but many of these children are left with the baggage of temporal values. The world is full of people who are making a good living but living poor lives. Don't doom your children to such emptiness. Instead, leave them with a legacy of grace-giving.

Leave your children with a legacy of grace-giving.

Currently, the United States government is implementing financial structures and loans that will be left to our children to bear. It is not God's plan to leave a burden, but to leave biblical values to the next generation.

When my family first moved to Lancaster, we spent much time making renovations to the church building. We had two young children at the time who would often play at the church while we made repairs. I'll never forget the afternoon I walked into the auditorium and found my son Larry behind the pulpit, with his knees on a shelf in the pulpit to prop himself up high enough to see over the top. He was preaching to an imaginary congregation in the empty auditorium. Cute as he was, it was a powerful reminder to me of the importance of my example in the life of my son.

One of the greatest investments you make when you give is the investment of your example in the lives of your children. What a good reason to give! Your influence has a weight that no other person has in their lives. Your participation in God's economy will be observed and copied by your children. What an opportunity!

CHAPTER NINE

Other Believers Need My Example

Golfer Payne Stewart had won the U.S. Open twice, and yet, life seemed empty for him until he accepted Christ at a Baptist church in Florida. Shortly after his salvation, the Lord touched his heart to give $500,000.00 to his new church for their building program. A few months later, at the age of forty-two, he died in a tragic plane accident.

I have walked through the administration and classroom building towards which he gave. It is a memorial to Payne Stewart's faith in God, and it is a lasting example to his church of giving to the work of the Lord.

Each of us wields the power of influence. Our examples carry far greater weight than our words. To realize the power of influence, pause a moment to consider those who have influenced *you*. How has your life been shaped by your spouse, parents, friends, teachers, pastor, others in your church? Who do you look up to, and how has their influence molded your beliefs and actions?

When I consider early influences in my life, one of the first people who comes to mind is Granddad Chappell. A bean farmer in Cortez, Colorado, Granddad saw the need for a Bible-preaching church in his community and started one himself. He constructed the church building, won souls to Christ, and later invited a "trained" preacher to come as a full-time pastor. He was one of the hardest workers I have known, yet he had a tender heart towards the Lord and loved God's Word with a passion.

Granddad was also one of the most generous givers I have ever known. His dad, my great-granddad, had started the farm when the government was awarding 160-acre homesteads. When Granddad took over the farm, he began increasing its size. As the Lord prospered his harvests, he purchased more and more acres of land. Even though more land meant more work for Granddad, he willingly expanded. Why? Because he wanted to have more resources to give. Granddad gave hundreds of thousands of dollars to the Lord's work over the years.

I praise the Lord for my granddad's godly influence that provided a powerful example of generosity and gave me a desire to serve the Lord as a pastor. I want the Lord to use *my* example as a positive influence in the lives of others as well.

Influence itself is a stewardship, an opportunity entrusted to you by God to impact others for Him and to direct others to live for Him. Don't squander this trust of influence—use it to further the work of the Lord!

My Priorities Set an Example

A missionary in Africa began teaching the young Christians in his church about tithing. The next morning, the missionary heard a knock at his door. When he opened it, he found a young African husband standing with a fishing pole in one hand and a fish in the other. "Here's my tithe," he said simply.

"Where are the rest of your fish?" the surprised missionary asked.

"Oh, they're still in the river. I just wanted to bring God His first."

Anyone could see where this growing young Christian's priorities fell!

Your true priorities are not necessarily those you would list on paper; rather, they are manifested through your actions. What you do reveals what is most important to you. What do those who know you see in your life to indicate that God's economy is your highest financial priority? Where does the first part of your paycheck go?

A temptation for those who have not experienced the blessings of living on God's economy is to give God what is left at the *end* of their paycheck. Before giving to God, they pay all of their bills—housing, electric, water, vehicle, phone, etc.—and then they see what is left at the end to give to God.

This method of giving reveals skewed priorities, and it presents a skewed testimony for other believers. Proverbs 3:9 instructs, *"Honour the LORD with thy substance, and with the **firstfruits** of all thine increase."* When we obey this verse and give to God before paying our other financial commitments, our example accomplishes two objectives.

First, it honors the Lord by demonstrating that we really believe He is worthy of our best. God is worthy of first place in every part of our lives, including our finances, and our example should clearly proclaim God's worthiness. Giving is an act of worship.

Influence itself is a stewardship.

Second, giving to God first gives God the opportunity to bless the remainder of our finances. He can do much better at stretching ninety percent than we can do with one hundred percent!

When my wife Terrie and I were dating, we agreed that the first ten percent of any income we received would be immediately designated to the Lord. As we worked on developing a budget, we quickly saw that living by this conviction was clearly not possible, and we wondered how we could tithe and still make our finances work.

By God's grace, we held to that commitment, and God *always* provided for our needs. The times of proving have been opportunities to solidify our commitment to honor and trust the Lord.

The exciting part of tithing is that it requires faith. When you worship God through the faith expressed in your tithing, He not only meets your needs (as He has always done for Terrie and me), but He increases your faith as well! And He uses your example to increase the faith of others.

My Sacrifice Sets an Example

During World War II, hundreds of thousands of young men made themselves available to pay the ultimate sacrifice in defense of freedom. One such young man was Private David Webster, a paratrooper of E. Company, 101st Airborne.

Apparently, David's mother was quite concerned for her son, for in a letter to her, David wrote, "Stop worrying about me. I joined the parachutists to fight. I intend to fight. If necessary, I shall die fighting, but don't worry about this because no war can be won without young men dying. Those things which are precious are saved only by sacrifice."

Others see what is most precious to you by observing those things for which you sacrifice. Our willingness to sacrifice is a reflection of our priorities—we give for that which is important to us.

You will remember from chapter 2 of this book that it was the sacrifice of the Macedonian Christians that enabled Paul to encourage the Corinthian Christians to give

(2 Corinthians 8:1–6). Would the example of your sacrifice motivate other believers to give?

My Consistency Sets an Example

The weightiest example is not always the loudest one, but, rather, it is the most consistent one. This is one reason it is important that our giving is not sporadic, but scheduled.

Paul instructed the Corinthian believers to regularly give on the first day of the week. *"Now concerning the collection for the saints, as I have given order to the churches of Galatia, even so do ye. Upon the first day of the week let every one of you lay by him in store, as God hath prospered him…"* (1 Corinthians 16:1–2).

I'm not against impulsive giving, if the impulse is from the Holy Spirit, but we must maintain a plan to give regularly.

In addition to regularly scheduled weekly offerings, special offerings for specific needs were common in Bible times. Moses collected an offering for the construction of the tabernacle (Exodus 35:5); David collected an offering for the construction of the temple (1 Chronicles 29:5); the churches of Macedonia collected an offering to relieve the financial needs of persecuted Christians (2 Corinthians 8:4).

Make the tithe the first item on your budget, and as you grow in grace, budget greater giving as well. Let your consistency in giving prove to others the sufficiency of God's grace.

Charles Spurgeon once remarked, "A man's life is always more forcible than his speech. When men take stock of him they reckon his deeds as dollars and his words as pennies. If his life and doctrine disagree, the mass of onlookers accept his practice and reject his preaching."

Let your consistency in giving prove to others the sufficiency of God's grace.

Are you utilizing the full value of your example, or are you settling for a "penny example"? Is your testimony a "words only" example, or do you lead through your actions?

Through your example, you can accomplish far more for the cause of Christ than is possible with only your resources. You can be the catalyst that propels others into the joys of living on God's economy.

CHAPTER TEN

I Want to Hear God Say, "Well Done!"

A film team approached the residents of a Florida home to obtain permission to use their front lawn for a car chase in a show. They needed a large lawn with an impressive house in the background, and this residence was perfect.

The team explained carefully that the car chase would involve the lawn being ripped up and the shrubs severely damaged. "No problem," the excited residents assured the team, "it will be just fine." They were blindly enthralled with the opportunity to have their home appear on prime time television.

All was fine until a few days later when a concerned neighbor called the owner of the house—who lived in New York. The residents, who gave permission for the filming, were renters, not owners.

There is an immense difference between an owner and a renter. The difference can best be explained in two words: rights and responsibilities. Owners have rights, but renters have responsibilities.

Our role in God's economy is that of a renter, or a manager. God has entrusted us with the responsibility of managing the resources with which He has provided us. And one day, we will each give an account to the Lord for our management of His resources. When I give my report, I long to hear the Lord say, "Well done, Paul!"

Multiply the Resources Entrusted to You

Jesus, in Matthew 25:14–30, told the parable of the talents to illustrate the principle of accountability. In this parable, a man called his servants and explained that he would be traveling for an extended period of time. He assigned each of them the responsibility of managing a portion of his assets while he was gone.

To one man, he assigned five talents (a *talent* was a piece of currency worth about twenty years' wages), to another two talents, and to another one talent. Jesus explained that the difference in the amounts reflected the varying abilities of each servant. The master gave them no more than he knew they could successfully manage.

When the owner returned, he asked his servants to give an account of how they had handled his resources. Two of the servants had doubled their master's money. As they reported on the interest they had earned, the master individually praised their faithfulness with the words, "*Well done, good and faithful servant…*" (Matthew 25:23).

One of the servants, however, had neglected to multiply his master's money. Instead, he hid it in the ground, not willing to take the risk of investment. This action angered the master, and he sternly condemned the servant's lack of responsibility with the words, "*Thou wicked and slothful servant…*" (Matthew 25:26).

Like the owner of the talents in this parable, our Lord has entrusted each of us with the responsibility of multiplying the resources He has given to us. He expects us not to simply *keep*, but to *multiply* the resources He has given to us. Let's briefly examine four ways we can multiply:

First, Scripture teaches us to **work diligently.** "*Wealth gotten by vanity shall be diminished: but he that gathereth by labour shall increase*" (Proverbs 13:11).

"Get rich quick schemes" are not God's method of multiplication. He blesses the diligence of a faithful, hard worker. As a Christian, you should be the most diligent and proactive worker at your job. Especially in a time of global economic recession, diligence is vital to make your employer successful and your job more secure.

Second, Scripture teaches us to **steward efficiently.** "*When they were filled, he said unto his disciples, Gather up the fragments that remain, that nothing be lost*" (John 6:12).

Even Jesus practiced thriftiness in gathering up the fragments of bread and fish He had multiplied.

As the age-old adage says, "A penny saved is a penny earned." Thriftiness allows us to multiply our resources that we might have more to give. Thriftiness differs from stinginess in that thriftiness is the practice of making personal sacrifices that one might have more to give, whereas stinginess is withholding from giving that one might have more for himself.

Third, Scripture teaches us to **invest wisely.** "*A gracious woman retaineth honour: and strong men retain riches*" (Proverbs 11:16).

Some people work to make money, some people make money work for them, and some people make money work for eternity's sake. This is the greatest investment.

Giving to God's work is a protected investment—the dividends are stored "*in heaven, where neither moth nor rust doth corrupt, and where thieves do not break through nor steal*" (Matthew 6:20).

Fourth, Scripture teaches us to **give generously.** "*There is that maketh himself rich, yet hath nothing: there is that maketh himself poor, yet hath great riches*" (Proverbs 13:7).

To those who do not understand God's ways, the idea of giving as part of a strategy to increase is a complete contradiction. We who understand the value of eternal investments and believe the truths of God's promises know that generous giving is one of the greatest ways to multiply God's resources.

God has designed us to be rivers, not reservoirs and channels, not containers. It is a delight to be the conduit through which God distributes His blessings.

"*But this I say, He which soweth sparingly shall reap also sparingly; and he which soweth bountifully shall reap also bountifully. Every man according as he purposeth in his heart, so let him give; not grudgingly, or of necessity: for God loveth a cheerful giver*" (2 Corinthians 9:6–7).

We could choose to spend our lives earning and hoarding wealth, but on the day we stand before Christ to give an account for how we handled His resources, we will regret our decision. How much better it is to spend our lives investing in God's economy!

As a pastor, I've been to many deathbeds to try to give encouragement and comfort. I've been personally blessed by the joy of Christians who had poured out their lives for their Lord and eagerly anticipated meeting Him face to face. I've also shared in the grief of Christians who sorrowed over a wasted life lived for self. I've heard Christians who were nearing Heaven say with a sigh, "I wish I had given more to the work of the Lord," but I have never heard a departing Christian say, "I wish I had not given so much to the work of the Lord."

> *God has designed us to be rivers, not reservoirs and channels, not containers.*

Living with the reminder of accountability motivates us to invest in God's economy. In the day we hear our Lord say, "Well done, good and faithful servant," nothing else will matter.

Live for Eternal Values

Real riches are not amassed here on earth; they are stored in Heaven. Attempting to gather riches here brings a deep soul-poverty.

John and Isobel Kuhn served as missionaries for many years in China. Once while the Kuhns were on furlough, a woman remarked to Isobel, "I care about nothing save my house and my garden. My house and my garden are my life." Isobel later wrote about this statement, "I thought how dreadfully poor she had made herself." In wrapping herself in her house and her garden, this lady had missed out on the true riches of living for God and investing in God's economy.

This is not to say that temporal wealth is wrong. As one person commented, "it is not wrong to own things as long as things do not own us!" Paul warned, not against money (for money can be a tool for the Lord), but against the *love* of money: *"For the love of money is the root of all evil: which while some coveted after, they have erred from the faith, and pierced themselves through with many sorrows"* (1 Timothy 6:10).

Notice that those who love money "pierce themselves through with many sorrows." Many are the wounds self-inflicted through the love of money. This list would include broken marriages, neglected children, wasted years consumed by temporal gain, resources frivolously thrown to the winds of sinful pleasures, and a host of other griefs.

Some people feel more important when they have more things. But in reality, they reduce their significance by attaching it to their possessions. Jesus explained that a man's life is much more than what he owns: *And he said unto them, Take heed, and beware of covetousness: for a man's life consisteth not in the abundance of the things which he possesseth*" (Luke 12:15).

If there is anything the principle of accountability should tell us, it is, "Live with eternal values." Don't allow yourself to become so focused on the here and now that you miss what really matters.

George W. Truett, a well-known Baptist pastor, was invited by a wealthy Texan to dinner on his ranch. After the meal, the host brought Pastor Truett outside to see the ranch. The property this man owned stretched as far as the eye could see in every direction. "Twenty-five years ago I had nothing," the man bragged, "but now, everything you can see is mine."

To the north were oil fields with working wells. To the south were fields of golden grain almost ready for harvest.

To the east were herds of beef cattle. To the west was a forest of timber.

Pastor Truett responded with a finger pointing heavenward and the question, "But how much do you have in that direction?"

"I never thought of that," the man confessed.

Invest your life, your time, your energy, and your resources in eternity.

Our Opportunity to Say "Thank You"

One day we will see Jesus face to face. We will see His hands that were nail-scarred for us. We will look into the eyes that were once thorn-shadowed and filled with unimaginable pain. We will understand as never before both the awfulness of the price He paid for our redemption and His exceeding great love for us. Our overwhelming passion at that moment will be to say "thank You," but there will be no words with which we can express the depth of our gratitude.

Yet God has provided a way for us, at that moment, to express gratefulness to Him. In God's economy, the eternal investments we make *now* will be translated into crowns that we can cast at the feet of Jesus. This act of humble, grateful worship will be our answer to the words "Well done." It will be our opportunity to demonstrate our gratefulness to Christ who gave His all for us.

If the Lord were to return today, are you ready to show Him your ledger, to give an account? Are you living in light of eternity? Are you managing what He has given you wisely?

God, just as the master in Jesus' parable, has entrusted each of us with different resources. The single quality the master in the parable praised was faithfulness. We may all have different amounts of resources, but we can all be faithful with what we have. "*Moreover it is required in stewards, that a man be found faithful*" (1 Corinthians 4:2).

*In God's economy, the eternal investments we make **now** will be translated into crowns that we can cast at the feet of Jesus.*

In God's economy, faithfulness will be rewarded with words of praise from God Himself: "*…Well done, thou good and faithful servant: thou hast been faithful over a few things, I will make thee ruler over many things: enter thou into the joy of thy lord*" (Matthew 25:21).

Conclusion

And so we see ten reasons to place our financial hope in the promises of God. They are:

1. Christ's Sacrifice Compels Me to Give.
2. The Example of First Century Christians Challenges Me to Give
3. Jesus Instructs Me to Give
4. Giving Produces Joy
5. My Commitment to Christ Calls Me to Give
6. The Mission of My Church is Worthy of My Investment
7. Giving Positions Me for God's Blessings
8. My Children Will Follow My Example
9. Other Believers Need My Example
10. I Want to Hear God Say, "Well Done!"

As the children of Israel prepared to give for the construction of the temple, David challenged the people to "...*be strong, and do it*" (1 Chronicles 28:10).

If you gaze long at the ups and downs of world economic systems, you will falter in your faith and neglect the grace of giving. If, however, you concentrate on the mighty promises of God and the security of living on God's economy, you will "be strong, and do it."

World economies shift and crumble, but God's economy is sure and rewarding. You may not be able to afford to give by world economic standards, but living on God's economy reveals that you can't afford *not* to give!

God created us and calls us to honor Him—to give back to Him a portion of what He gives to us. And in response, He promises to meet our needs according to His riches in glory. Our giving shows our gratitude for what He has done in the past, it shows our priority is on Him in the present, and it shows that our hope is on Him in the future.

So I challenge you—"just do it!" Enter the joys of living on God's economy!

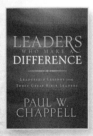

Visit us online

strivingtogether.com

dailyintheword.org

wcbc.edu

lancasterbaptist.org

paulchappell.com